Animals

Eli Rector

Vidoqo Books

2016

First Edition

ISBN: 978-1-365-54819-2

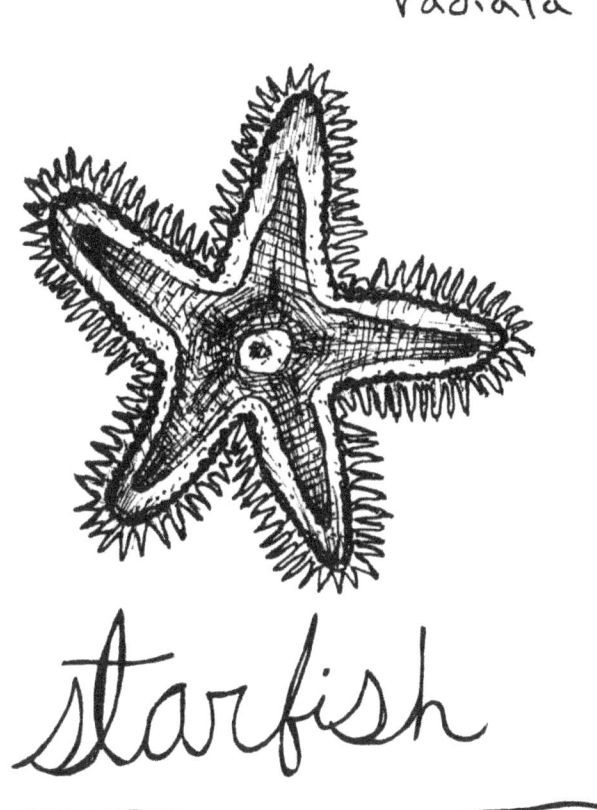

radiata

starfish

radiata

jellyfish

bilateria

chordate

sea squirt

chordate

lancelet

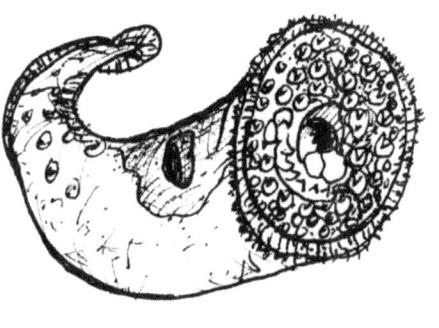

deuterostomia
jawless fish

lamprey

deuterostomia
cartilaginous fish

shark

deuterostomia
bony fish

oarfish

deuterostomia
amphibians

toad

deuterostomia
reptiles

turtle

deuterostomia
birds
neoaves

crane

deuterostomia
birds
galloanserae

jungle fowl

deuterostomia
birds
paleognathae

ostrich

mammalia

deuterostomia
mammals
Prototheria

platypus

deutero stomia
mammals
theriformes
marsupials

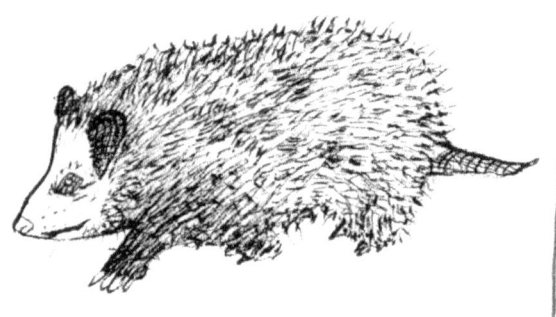

opposum

deuterostomia
mammals
theriformes
placentals
afrotheria

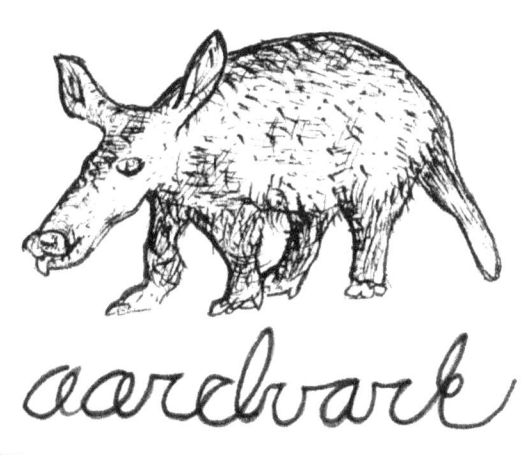

aardvark

deuterostomia
mammals
theriformes
placentals
boreoeutheria
gliriformes

beaver

deuterostomia
mammals
theriformes
placentals
boreoeutheria
eurchonta
primates

human

deuterostomia
mammals
theriformes
placentals
Xenarthra

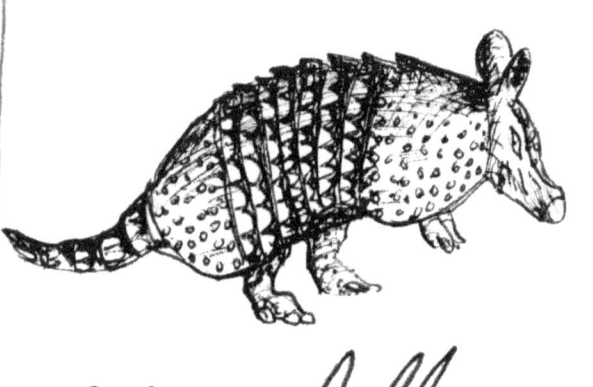

armadillo

protostomia
arthropoda
insecta
hymenoptera

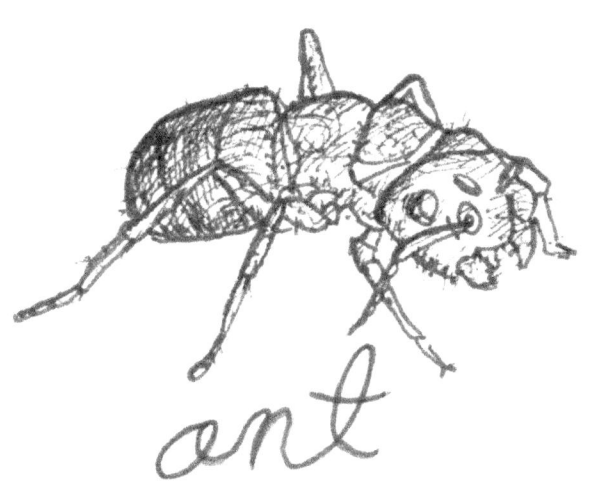

ant

arthropoda

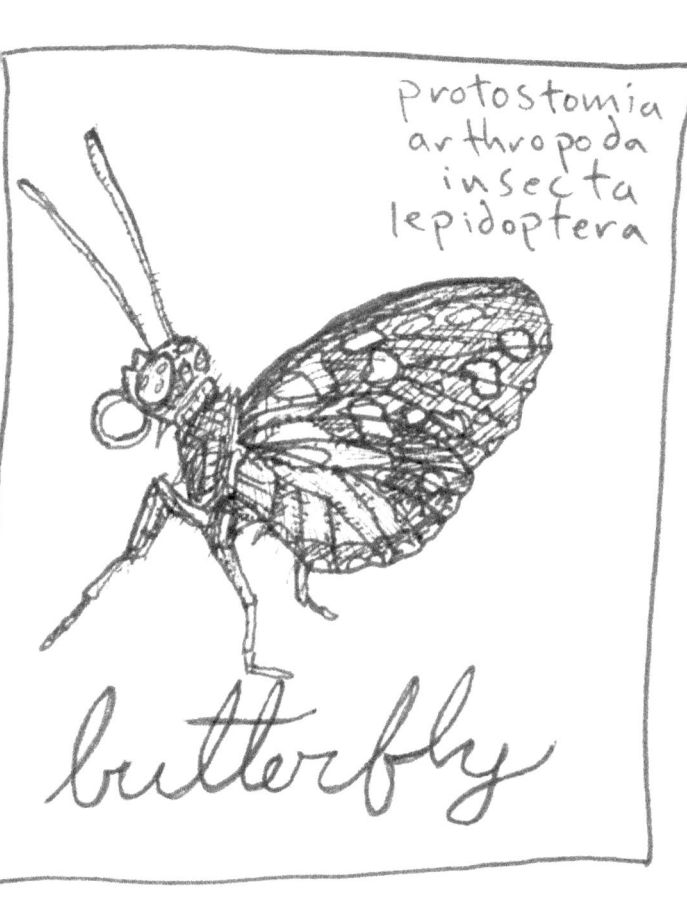

protostomia
arthropoda
insecta
lepidoptera

butterfly

protostomia
arthropoda
insecta
coleoptera

beetle

protostomia
arthropoda
insecta
diptera

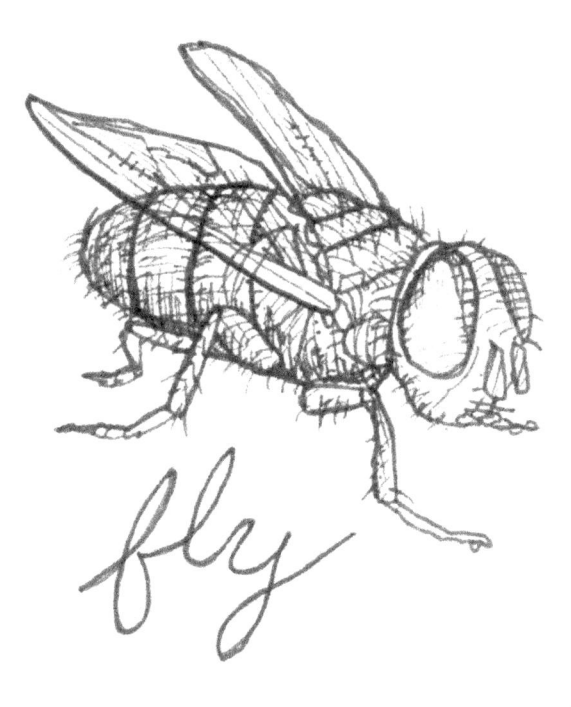

fly

protostomia
arthropoda
chelicerata
arachnida

spider

protostomia
arthropoda
chelicerata
merostomata

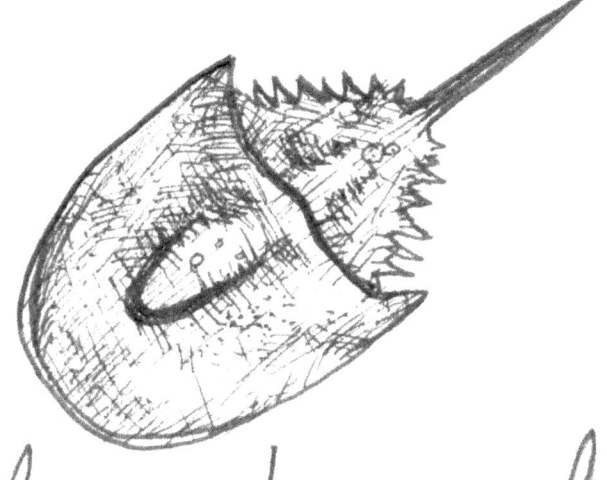

horseshoe crab

protostomia
arthropoda
myriapoda
chilopoda

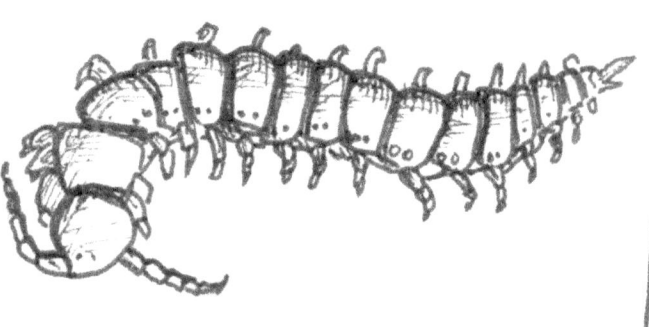

centipede

mollusca

protostomia
arthropoda
crustacea
maxillopoda

barnacle

protostomia
arthropoda
crustacea
malacostraca

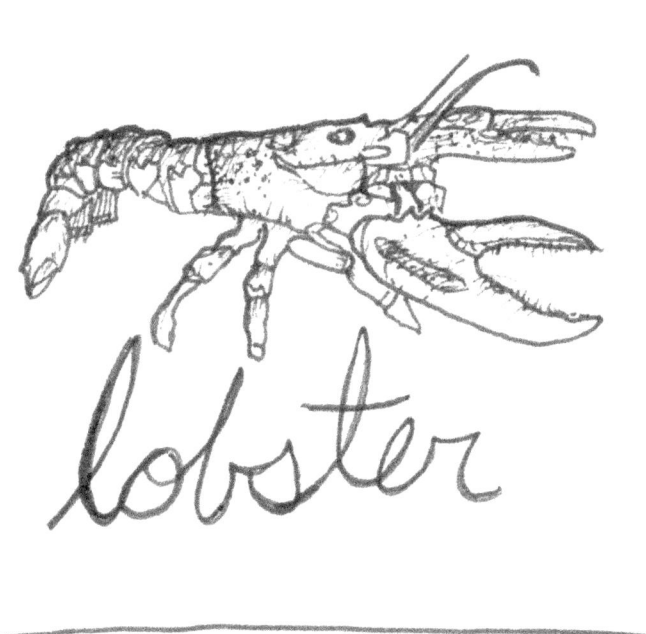

lobster

protostomia
mollusca
polyplacophora

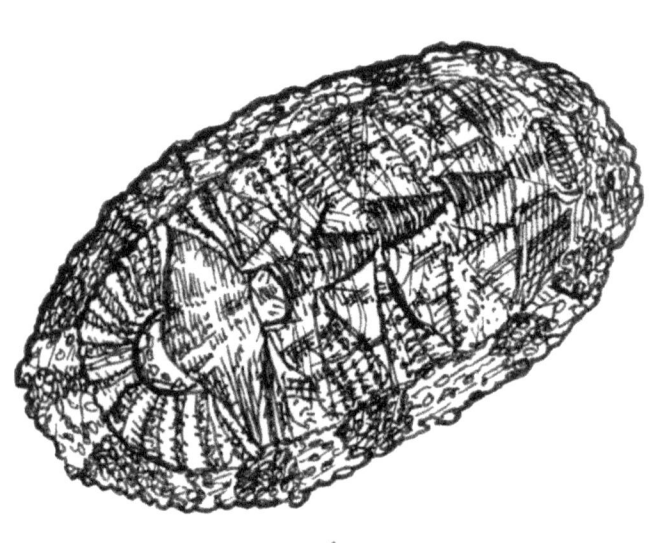

chiton

protostomia
mollusca
gastropoda

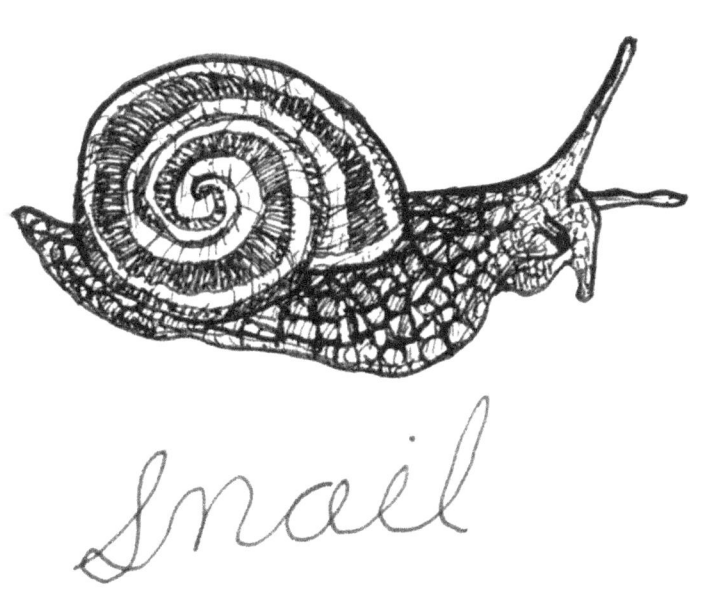

Snail

protostomia
mollusca
gastropoda

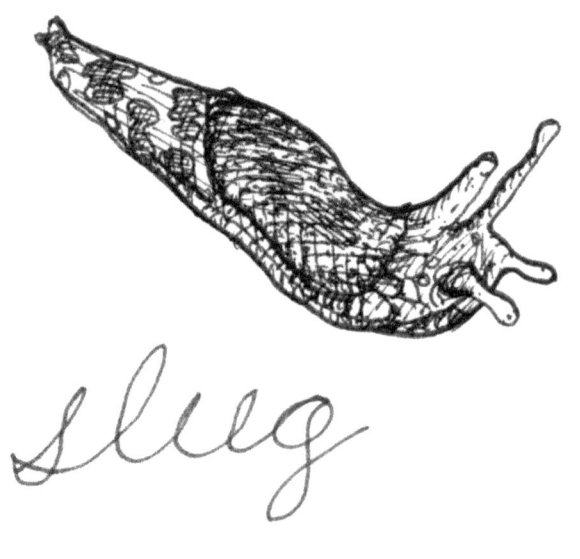

slug

protostomia
mollusca
gastropoda

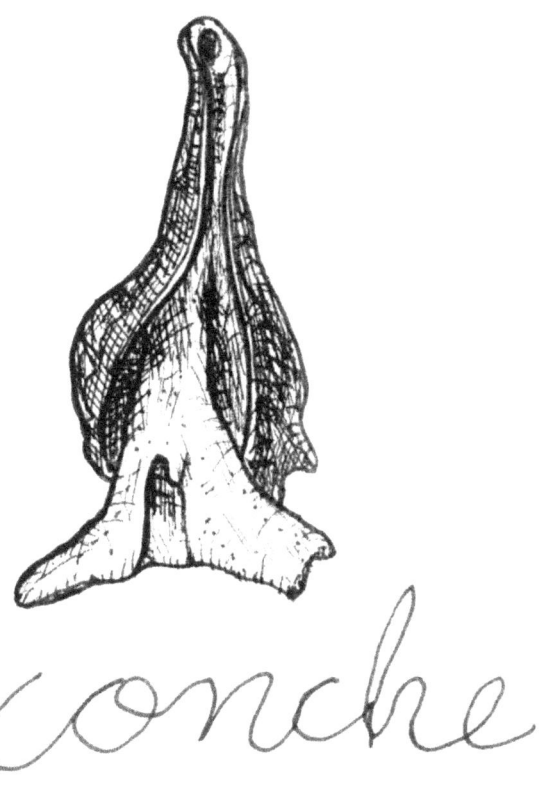

conche

protostomia
mollusca
cephalopoda

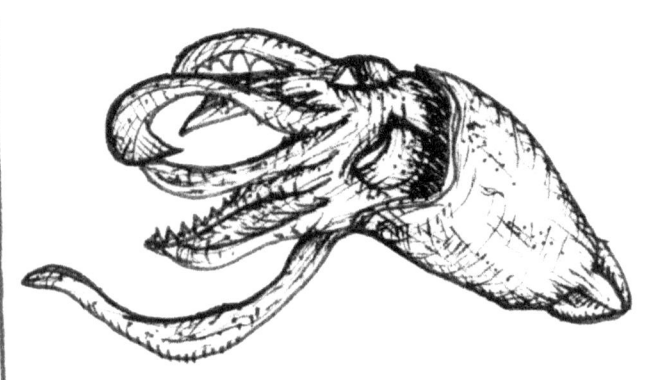

squid

protostomia
mollusca
cephalopoda

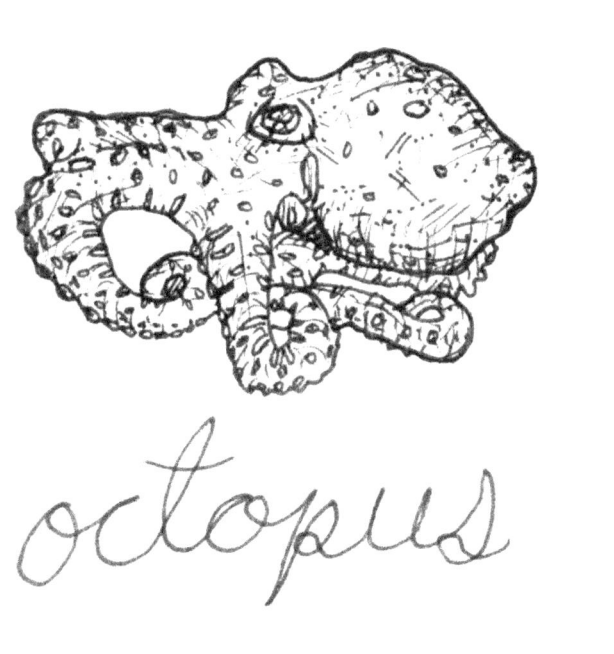

octopus

protostomia
mollusca
cephalopoda

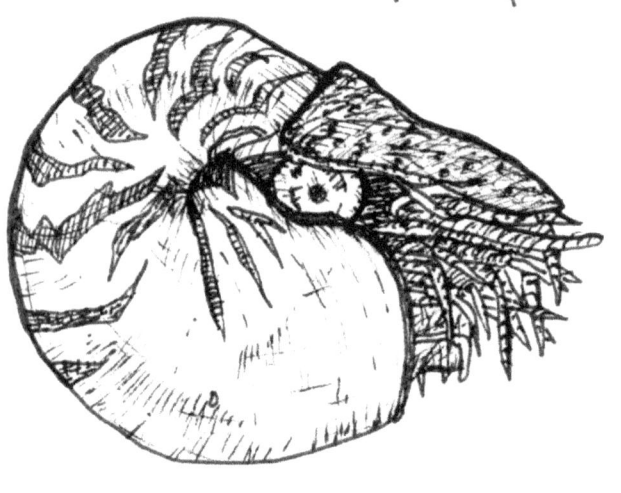

nautilus

protostomia
mollusca
bivalvia

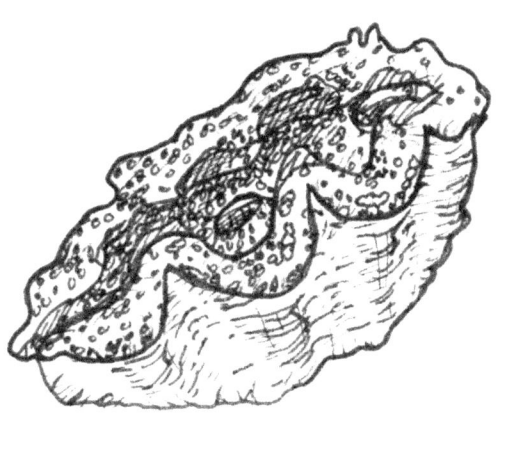

clam

protostomia
mollusca
bivalvia

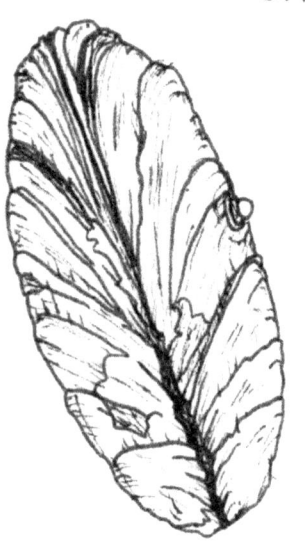

mussel